THE EVOLUTION OF SOCIAL MEDIA

From Myspace to TikTok

Philipp Frühwirth

CONTENTS

THE EARLY DAYS: THE EMERGENCE OF SOCIAL MEDIA

Social media has become an integral part of our daily lives. It allows us to connect with friends, family, and people from different parts of the world. But, have you ever wondered how it all started? The history of social media dates back more than two decades, and it has come a long way since then.

The concept of social media began in the late 1970s with the invention of Usenet. Usenet was a messaging system where users could post messages, read and respond to them. It was mainly used by academics and researchers to share information and collaborate on projects.

In the 1980s, Bulletin Board Systems (BBS) emerged as the precursor to social media. BBSs were similar to Usenet, but they required users to dial-in using a modem. This allowed people to share information, files, and engage in online discussions.

The birth of the internet in the 1990s paved the way for the introduction of social networking sites. The first social networking site was Six Degrees, launched in 1997. It allowed users to create a profile, connect with friends, and send messages. It was the first platform to use the term "friends" to describe connections between users.

In 2002, Friendster emerged as the first massive social networking site. It allowed users to discover new friends based on their interests and connections. Friendster's success paved the way for the introduction of other social networking sites such as MySpace and LinkedIn.

In 2004, Mark Zuckerberg launched Facebook, which is now the largest social networking site in the world. Initially, Facebook was only available to college students, but it soon expanded to other universities, high schools, and then, the general public.

Twitter, a microblogging site, was launched in 2006. It allowed users to tweet short messages of up to 140 characters. Twitter has become a popular platform to share news, information, and connect with celebrities.

In conclusion, social media has come a long way since the early days of Usenet and BBS. Today, social media is an essential part of our lives, and it has changed the way we interact and communicate with others. The evolution of social media has led to the emergence of different platforms, making it easier to connect and share our lives with others around the world.

THE EVOLUTION OF
SOCIAL MEDIA

Social media has come a long way since the early days of AOL chat rooms and MySpace. The evolution of social media has been driven largely by advances in technology, changes in consumer behavior, and the emergence of new platforms with different features and capabilities.

In the early days, social media was primarily used for online communication and connecting with others who shared common interests. As technology advanced, so too did social media platforms, with the addition of multimedia capabilities, improved algorithms, and more interactive interfaces.

One of the biggest changes in social media has been the shift from text-based communication to more visual forms of content, including images, videos, and livestreaming. This has been largely driven by the popularity of platforms like Instagram and YouTube, which prioritize visual content over text in their algorithms.

Another major evolution in social media has been the rise of algorithms and artificial intelligence. These technologies help determine what content users see in their feeds, based on factors such as engagement, relevance, and user behavior. This has led to a more personalized user experience, with content tailored to individual preferences and interests.

In recent years, social media has also become increasingly mobile-focused, with many users accessing platforms primarily through their smartphones. As a result, platforms have had to adapt their interfaces and functionality to better suit mobile users, such as simplified navigation and the ability to post and consume content on the go.

New platforms have also emerged with different features and focuses, such as TikTok and Twitch. TikTok prioritizes short-form video content and user-generated challenges, while Twitch is primarily focused on livestreaming gameplay and esports content.

Overall, the evolution of social media has been driven by a combination of technological advancements, consumer behavior changes, and the emergence of new platforms with different capabilities. It remains to be seen what the future of social media will look like, but one thing is certain - it will continue to evolve and adapt to the changing needs and preferences of users.

FROM AOL CHAT ROOMS
TO FACEBOOK

In the early days of the internet, people communicated through chat rooms and instant messaging services. One of the earliest examples of this was AOL Instant Messenger, which allowed people to connect and chat with others online in real-time. This was revolutionary at the time, as it allowed people to communicate with others from all around the world without having to be in the same physical location.

As technology evolved, so did social media. In 2004, a young Mark Zuckerberg launched a website called "TheFacebook" from his dorm room at Harvard University. At the time, it was simply a way for Harvard students to connect with each other online. However, it quickly gained popularity and expanded to other universities across the United States.

Soon, anyone with a valid email address could create a Facebook account, and the platform grew rapidly in popularity. Facebook allowed people to connect with old friends and make new ones, share photos and videos, and update their status to let others know what they were up to. It was an all-in-one platform that quickly replaced the need for other social networking sites like MySpace and Friendster.

In addition to connecting with friends and family, Facebook also became a platform for businesses and organizations to advertise their products and services. This helped to turn the social networking site into a money-making machine, making Zuckerberg one of the youngest billionaires in the world.

But Facebook was not without its controversies. Over the years, the platform has faced criticism for its handling of user data and privacy concerns. The company has also been accused of allowing fake news to spread on the platform, leading to increased scrutiny and calls for regulation.

Despite these issues, Facebook remains one of the most popular social networking sites in the world. With over 2.8 billion monthly active users, it has become an essential tool for staying in touch with loved ones and staying up-to-date with current events. And it all started from a simple website created in a dorm room.

THE RISE OF SOCIAL NETWORKING SITES

As the internet age continued to evolve, online communication and interactions grew. By the early 2000s, the concept of social networking sites began making waves online. These sites brought people together, allowing them to connect from anywhere in the world.

Classmates.com was one of the first social networking sites to gain traction in the late 1990s. The site allowed people to connect with their former classmates and friends, paving the way for more social networking sites to emerge.

In 2002, Friendster entered the scene, allowing users to create profiles, add friends, and share content. The site quickly gained a massive following, especially among younger users.

However, Friendster's success was short-lived as technical issues and user experience problems led to a decline in popularity. From Friendster's ashes, new social networking sites emerged, such as MySpace, which became the world's largest social networking site by 2006, with over 100 million registered users.

MySpace allowed users to customize their profiles, adding music, images, and other content. It was a perfect platform for musicians, bands, and other artists to promote and build their fan base. However, by the late 2000s, MySpace's popularity, too, waned as newer and better social networking sites emerged.

In 2004, Facebook arrived on the scene, initially, starting as a social networking site for college students. However, it quickly became open to everyone, and its userbase grew rapidly.

The design and user experience of Facebook were far superior to that of its predecessors, and it offered features like news feeds, a like button, and a clean user interface. It became the dominant social networking site worldwide, with over two billion registered users today.

Other social networking sites followed Facebook's lead, such as Twitter, Instagram, Snapchat, and LinkedIn. Each site has its own unique features and audience, allowing users to connect with different types of people and communities.

These social networking sites transformed the way we interact with each other, making it possible to connect with anyone from anywhere in the world. The rise of social networking sites has undoubtedly reshaped the landscape of communication and social interaction in the 21st century.

THE EMERGENCE OF BLOGGING

Blogging, a term derived from the phrase "weblog," was introduced to the online world in the late 1990s. The first blog creator was links.net inventor Justin Hall, who started his blog in 1994. The concept of blogging came from the idea of individuals sharing their thoughts and opinions online, with the hope of reaching a wider audience. However, the use of blogs eventually evolved beyond just personal musings to professional writing and journalism.

In the early days of blogging, users could only post text and images, and they had to learn coding and website design to create their blogs. However, with the emergence of platforms such as Blogger and WordPress, anyone could start a blog with minimal technical knowledge. These platforms made it easy for people to express their beliefs and share ideas with the world.

One of the key use cases of blogging has been political commentary. During the George Bush and John Kerry presidential race in 2004, blogs emerged as a platform for political discourse. Bloggers such as Andrew Sullivan and Markos Moulitsas Zuniga utilized their platforms to voice their political opinions, resulting in increased political engagement among the American electorate.

As blogging continued to gain popularity, individuals and businesses began utilizing it as a marketing tool. Businesses could use blogs to share product information, and improve search engine optimization (SEO) while simultaneously engaging with customers. The content produced by bloggers could also be used for guest posting on other sites, with links back to their personal blog, thus increasing their reach and following.

Blogging has also provided a platform for writers and journalists to showcase their work. New journalists could create their personal blog, build an audience and showcase their writing, leading to job offers from larger news organizations. Even major publications such as The New York Times, CNN and Forbes now have their blogs, further cementing the role of blogging in the digital landscape.

In conclusion, blogging has provided individuals and businesses with a platform to share their thoughts and ideas in a cost-effective and versatile manner. Its uses have evolved from being a personal source of creative expression to a marketing tool for businesses and a platform for political commentary, making it an essential component of today's social media landscape.

THE IMPACT OF TWITTER

Twitter is one of the most well-known and widely-used social media platforms, with over 330 million monthly active users as of 2021. It was founded in 2006 by Jack Dorsey, Biz Stone, and Evan Williams, and has since then become a powerful platform for communication and information-sharing.

Twitter's format is unique compared to other social networks; users can post "tweets" - short messages of up to 280 characters - that are displayed on their profile and can also be seen by anyone who follows them. Twitter has become a crucial means of communication for individuals, businesses, and even governments.

One of the most significant impacts of Twitter has been its ability to break news and spread information quickly. Because tweets can be posted instantly and seen by a large audience, it has become a go-to platform for journalists, news organizations, and even individuals on the ground during a breaking news event. During natural disasters, terrorist attacks, or other global events, Twitter often becomes the fastest and most reliable source of information.

Politicians and other public figures have also taken to Twitter as a means of communicating with their constituents or fans. The direct nature of the platform allows them to bypass traditional media and speak directly to their followers, oftentimes in real-time. Former U.S. President Donald Trump, for example, famously used Twitter to communicate and express his views throughout his presidency, with his tweets often becoming headlines themselves.

Twitter has also become a platform for social activism and political movements. The hashtag has become a powerful tool for organizing and spreading messages across the site, with movements like #MeToo and #BlackLivesMatter gaining momentum and attention through Twitter.

However, Twitter has also been criticized for its role in spreading false information, as well as for issues of harassment and trolling on the platform. The company has taken steps to address these issues, such as implementing strict policies on hate speech and working to prevent the spread of false information.

Overall, Twitter has had a significant impact on how we communicate and share information, becoming a powerful tool for breaking news, political communication, and social activism. Its unique format and ability to connect individuals and organizations from around the world have made it a vital part of the social media landscape.

THE INTRODUCTION
OF HASHTAGS

In 2007, Twitter introduced a simple concept that would revolutionize the way people use and search for content on social media: hashtags. A hashtag is a word or phrase preceded by the pound sign (#), used to group and categorize tweets and posts on various social media platforms. The use of hashtags quickly became popular on Twitter and spread to other platforms like Facebook and Instagram.

The idea for the hashtag came from Chris Messina, a product designer and user experience consultant for tech startups. Messina initially proposed the use of hashtags on Twitter as an easy way for users to search for content related to a particular topic. He tweeted: "how do you feel about using # (pound) for groups. As in #barcamp [msg]?"

The idea quickly caught on, and it wasn't long until hashtags were being used by millions of people around the world. Today, hashtags are an essential part of social media conversations, used to categorize posts, find relevant content, and track trending topics.

Hashtags have become an integral part of social media marketing strategies as well. Brands use hashtags to build their social media presence and increase engagement with their audience. Some of the most memorable hashtag marketing campaigns include Coca-Cola's #ShareACoke, which encouraged customers to share pictures of Coca-Cola bottles with their friends on social media, and Nike's #justdoit, which has become synonymous with the brand's advertising campaigns.

The popularity of hashtags has also led to the emergence of social media influencers who specialize in creating content around specific hashtags. These individuals have built large followings by creating and sharing content related to popular hashtags, such as #fitspo, #foodporn, and #travelgram.

In recent years, hashtags have evolved beyond simple categorization tools. They now have their own subculture, with celebrities, memes, and political movements all having their own unique hashtags. Hashtags have been used to raise awareness and spark social and political movements, with #MeToo and #BlackLivesMatter being some of the most well-known examples.

In summary, the introduction of hashtags revolutionized the way people use and search for content on social media. They have become an essential part of social media conversations around the world, and have become an integral part of social media marketing strategies. They continue to evolve and have become a cultural phenomenon in their own right.

INSTAGRAM AND THE RISE
OF VISUAL STORYTELLING

In 2010, Instagram, a photo and video sharing app took the world by storm. With its easy-to-use functionalities and visually engaging platform, Instagram quickly became one of the most popular social media platforms. It currently boasts over one billion monthly active users and has revolutionized the way we tell stories online.

Instagram's emphasis on visual content holds a significant appeal to its users. It's been widely recognized that humans process visual information faster than any other type of information. This explains why visual content on Instagram tends to perform better than written posts. Instagram's implementation of Stories has only further enforced visual storytelling. Stories are short, ephemeral glimpses into a user's daily life. They can be decorated with a wide variety of interactive features like stickers and filters.

The visual storytelling trend on Instagram has also given rise to the influencer culture. Instagram influencers, people with large followings, collaborate with brands to promote their products. Because they create visually stunning content, they've become valuable to brands' marketing efforts. Many influencers have become household names and celebrities because of Instagram, and they're even able to earn a living through their content.

Instagram's primary focus on photos and videos has pushed it towards innovating creative ways to include text in posts. Hashtags are a prime example of this, and have become an essential component of Instagram. Hashtags were first introduced to Instagram in 2011 to help users discover content relevant to their interests. Implementing hashtags allowed users to make their content searchable and discoverable by people who weren't following them. Today, hashtags are used by individuals, businesses, and influencers to help expand the reach of their content.

In conclusion, Instagram has changed the way we capture and share moments in our lives. Its unique position as a visual storytelling platform has given rise to a new era of storytelling on social media, allowing us to connect with the world in an entirely different way. Instagram's impact on culture and marketing proves that visual storytelling is here to stay.

THE BIRTH OF SNAPCHAT

When it comes to the history of social media, Snapchat is a relative newcomer, having been founded in 2011 by Evan Spiegel and Bobby Murphy. What began as an app that allowed users to send self-deleting photos and videos to their friends quickly grew into a social media platform in its own right.

Snapchat's origins can be traced back to a class project at Stanford University, where Spiegel and Murphy were studying. Originally called "Picaboo," the app was intended to allow users to share photos that would disappear once viewed. The idea was inspired by Spiegel's experience of wishing to send a risqué photo to a friend without the fear of it being shared or saved. However, after initial tests with close friends showed a demand for the app, Picaboo was renamed and became available on the App Store in September 2011.

Snapchat quickly gained a reputation for being a platform focused on privacy and fleeting content. Unlike rival social media apps such as Facebook and Instagram, Snapchat allowed messages and media to be shared for a limited time only, with the sender able to set an expiration date for each piece of content.

However, Snapchat always had more to offer than just disappearing messages. One of the app's most popular features was "Stories," a series of photos and videos shared publicly and viewable for 24 hours. Stories allowed users to curate and share their experiences in real-time, often making use of Snapchat's quirky and playful filters and effects.

Snapchat's user base grew rapidly, particularly among younger demographics who were drawn to the app's unique features and sense of fun. By 2014, Snapchat had over 100 million daily active users, and it continued to expand its offerings with features such as "Discover," a platform for media companies to share stories and videos.

While Snapchat faced challenges from rival apps such as Instagram, which introduced its own version of Stories in 2016, the platform continued to innovate and develop new features. Today, Snapchat is used by millions of people around the world, with a range of offerings including augmented reality lenses, personalized Bitmoji avatars, and a range of filters and effects.

In many ways, Snapchat has been a game-changer in the social media landscape, offering a fresh and playful take on user-generated content. Its success has also highlighted the importance of privacy and trust in social media, with an emphasis on transparency and user control over what is shared and for how long.

PINTEREST: THE VIRTUAL PINBOARD

Launched in 2010, Pinterest is a visual discovery engine that allows users to save and discover ideas in the form of pins on virtual pinboards. The platform initially gained popularity among women as a way to curate their interests, but today it has a much broader appeal, with over 459 million active users worldwide.

Pinterest's success is largely due to its unique approach to social media. Unlike other platforms that focus on status updates, messaging, and building networks of contacts, Pinterest prioritizes visual content and discovery. Users browse boards created by others and save content that they find inspiring or useful. They can also follow specific boards or accounts to see curated content that matches their interests.

One of the keys to Pinterest's success is its algorithm, which prioritizes content that is relevant to users' interests. When a pin is saved, Pinterest uses machine learning to determine what that pin is about and then suggests similar content. This approach has made Pinterest a powerful tool for brand discovery and eCommerce. Companies can use the platform to showcase their products, generate leads, and drive sales.

Over the years, Pinterest has introduced new features to enhance the user experience. In 2013, it launched Promoted Pins, a form of advertising that lets brands promote their content to a wider audience. In 2017, they introduced Lens, a visual search tool that allows users to take a picture of an item and find similar images on Pinterest. They have also added e-commerce capabilities, enabling users to shop for products directly on the platform.

Pinterest has had to navigate some challenges as well, particularly around content moderation. The platform has had to deal with issues like the spread of misinformation and the promotion of harmful content. In response, Pinterest has implemented policies to promote accuracy and safety. For example, they have banned ads for weight loss products, restrict content related to harmful vaccine misinformation, and provide resources for users struggling with mental health issues.

Overall, Pinterest has become a popular and influential platform that is changing the way people discover and share ideas online. Its unique approach to social networking has made it a valuable marketing tool for businesses and a source of inspiration for millions of users.

LINKEDIN: THE PROFESSIONAL NETWORK

Launched in 2003, LinkedIn remains the leading professional social media site, boasting over 700 million members across 200 countries. The site is designed to connect professionals with colleagues, clients, and potential employers.

LinkedIn users create an online profile, highlighting their work history, education, skills, and achievements. The platform is used to build professional networks, search for job opportunities, and share industry insights.

One of the primary benefits of LinkedIn is the access it provides to a vast professional network. The platform is used to connect with potential clients, business partners, and prospective employers. LinkedIn also offers a feature called LinkedIn Groups, which allows users to connect with like-minded professionals in their industry.

LinkedIn has become an essential tool for recruitment and job searching. Employers and recruiters use the platform to search for candidates based on their skills and experience, and job seekers can also use LinkedIn to search for job opportunities and apply directly through the site.

In recent years, LinkedIn has expanded its features to include more content and news sharing capabilities. Users can now publish articles, share industry news and insights, and engage in discussions around specific topics.

LinkedIn's premium membership, called LinkedIn Premium, offers additional features such as enhanced search and communication tools, access to online courses, and more in-depth insights into profile visitors.

Overall, LinkedIn has revolutionized the way professionals connect, build networks, search for jobs, and share industry insights. Its continued growth and evolution ensure that it will remain a significant player in the professional social media landscape for years to come.

TWITCH: GAMING AND SOCIAL MEDIA

When it comes to online gaming and livestreaming, Twitch is undoubtedly the biggest name in the industry. The platform started out as a simple spin-off of Justin.tv, a general-purpose streaming site launched in 2007. In 2011, Twitch was officially launched as a separate platform focused entirely on live streaming video games.

At the time, video game live streaming was still a niche interest, and Twitch faced a lot of skepticism about whether there was even an audience for it. But as the years went on, the platform's popularity consistently grew, with the company reporting more than 100 million monthly active users in 2020.

One key to Twitch's success has been its integration with other social media platforms. Streamers can easily share their broadcasts on Twitter or Facebook, and viewers can follow their favorite streamers to receive notifications when they go live. Twitch has also made it easy for viewers to chat and interact with one another during streams, building a sense of community around the platform.

Another factor that has helped Twitch thrive is the rise of esports, or organized video game competitions. Twitch was an early leader in streaming esports events, and it has continued to invest heavily in the space. In 2018, Twitch signed a two-year deal worth $90 million to stream the popular esports league Overwatch League.

Of course, Twitch is not without its controversies. The platform has faced criticism for the way it handles moderation, with some streamers accused of engaging in harassment or making offensive comments on their streams. Twitch has also struggled with keeping up with the demands of its massive user base, with frequent service outages and long wait times for customer support.

Despite these challenges, Twitch remains a dominant force in the world of gaming and live video streaming. The platform has spawned a new generation of content creators and given rise to entirely new forms of entertainment. Whether you're a hardcore gamer or just looking for something fun to watch, there's something for everyone on Twitch.

THE ROLE OF YOUTUBE
IN SOCIAL MEDIA

It is hard to imagine a world without YouTube. The video-sharing platform has become an integral part of our lives, offering an endless stream of content on just about any topic you could imagine. It has also become one of the most influential social media platforms, with the power to make or break careers and affect social change. But how did YouTube come about, and what role has it played in the evolution of social media?

YouTube was launched in February 2005 by three former PayPal employees: Chad Hurley, Steve Chen, and Jawed Karim. The idea for the site came about when the trio had difficulty finding videos of Janet Jackson's infamous Super Bowl halftime show wardrobe malfunction. They realized that there was a need for a platform that made it easy for people to upload and share videos online. YouTube was born.

From the beginning, YouTube had a democratizing effect on media. Anyone with a camera and an internet connection could create and share content with a global audience. This gave rise to a new generation of content creators who built loyal followings by producing engaging, informative, and entertaining videos on a wide range of topics. In fact, YouTube has helped launch the careers of some of the biggest names in entertainment, music, and comedy, including Justin Bieber, Shawn Mendes, and Lilly Singh.

YouTube has also played a significant role in political and social activism. Videos of police brutality, environmental disasters, and political corruption have spread like wildfire on the platform, triggering public outrage and catalyzing protests and social movements. The #MeToo movement gained momentum on

YouTube, where survivors of sexual assault shared their stories and inspired others to do the same.

The platform has continued to evolve, adding features like live streaming, community tab, and YouTube Shorts to keep up with the changing demands of users. It has also faced criticism for the spread of misinformation and harmful content on the platform. However, YouTube remains an important part of social media, providing a space for people to connect, learn, and share information on a global scale.

THE INFLUENCE OF SOCIAL MEDIA ON POLITICS

Social media has become an essential platform in contemporary politics. Social media has influenced a variety of aspects, including the way that candidates and parties communicate with voters, how voters access data, and how they interact with public authorities. Political campaigns are increasingly incomplete without social media as it is an integral part.

In the present day, political campaigns will be incomplete without a social media presence. It is considered an essential tool for candidates to reach out to younger voters, streamline messages, and perform fundraising activities. With over 2.8 billion social media users globally, social media platforms such as Twitter, Facebook, and Instagram have proven to be powerful weapons for political campaigns.

Political parties and candidates leverage social media's immense user base to access potential supporters and opinions on their messages. A simple Facebook post or a tweet can reach millions of individuals in a matter of seconds. Social media has also enabled politicians to communicate with younger individuals, who tend to be more tech-savvy and likely to rely on social media for information. Political campaigns are therefore now focussed on creating content that is easily shareable on social media.

The impact of social media on politics has also created new opportunities for dialogue between policymakers and the public. Social media platforms have allowed politicians to remain connected with their constituents and address their concerns directly, thus making the government more accessible to the masses.

The trend of campaigning originated from traditional media that was manipulated and controlled by influential people. But now, social media has disintegrated this pattern, and campaigns now have a direct line of communication with people. Social media provides the ability to reach a large audience, enhances transparency in political associations, and makes communication between politicians and people more amiable.

However, social media's impact on politics can also lead to negativity such as increased polarization in political discourse, cyberbullying, the spread of misinformation, hacking and disinformation campaigns, particularly during election periods. Social media has also given rise to the growth of echo chambers, where people only interact with those who share their political beliefs, leading to a limited volume of public discourse.

In conclusion, social media platforms have transformed political campaigns, political communication, and political discourse. Everything from the way we communicate and share information to organizing voting blocs and fundraising has been impacted by social media. While it undoubtedly provides advantages, it can also have detrimental outcomes if not used correctly. Social media will likely continue to play an increasingly significant role in politics as its usage becomes more widespread around the globe.

SOCIAL MEDIA IN CRISIS COMMUNICATION

One of the most significant aspects of social media is its role in crisis communication. In today's hyper-connected world, social media has become a vital tool for governments, organizations, and individuals to communicate and disseminate critical information in times of crises. It has proven effective in managing disaster response, coordinating relief efforts, and providing updates during emergencies.

Social media platforms have become the primary source of news and updates during crises, from natural disasters to terrorist attacks. In 2019, a survey revealed that more than 60% of adults in the United States relied on social media for news during a crisis. Social media platforms such as Twitter, Facebook, and Instagram allow individuals to share real-time updates, photos, and videos of the event as it unfolds. This information can be extremely valuable in informing the public and helping responders to better understand the situation.

Social media is an essential component of crisis communication due to its speed, accessibility, and reach. It enables emergency responders, news media, and the public to receive information instantly in real-time, regardless of location. Social media has also made it possible for people to connect with relatives and friends during emergencies when traditional communication channels are disrupted.

In addition to being a channel for the dissemination of information, social media has also made it easier for organizations and governments to coordinate relief efforts. Social media platforms such as Facebook and Twitter allow for the quick mobilization of volunteers and donations by connecting people with individuals and organizations that need help. This can significantly reduce the time and effort required to coordinate and deploy resources during a crisis.

However, social media can also present challenges during crisis communication. False information can spread rapidly in times of crisis, leading to panic and confusion. It is essential to have a plan in place to verify information and ensure that only accurate information is being shared on social media. Additionally, social media can be used for nefarious purposes, including spreading misinformation or coordinating attacks.

Overall, social media has revolutionized crisis communication in many ways. It has become an essential tool for disseminating critical information, coordinating relief efforts, and connecting people during emergencies. As social media continues to evolve, it is essential to recognize its benefits and limitations in crisis communication and to develop strategies for mitigating potential risks.

THE DARK SIDE OF SOCIAL MEDIA: CYBERBULLYING

While social media has drastically transformed the way we communicate and connect with others, it has also given rise to a worrying phenomenon: cyberbullying. Cyberbullying refers to the use of technology, particularly social media platforms, to harm, harass or bully people. It has become a growing problem, especially among young people.

One of the main reasons cyberbullying is so prevalent is that it is easy to do anonymously. Cyberbullies can hide behind fake social media accounts or anonymous usernames, making it challenging to determine their identifications. They can create fake profiles or use other people's identities to harass or bully others. Furthermore, the distance provided by technology makes it easier for individuals to write things they might not say in person, which can exacerbate the issue.

Studies have shown that cyberbullying can have severe negative effects on mental health. Victims of cyberbullying may experience anxiety, depression, and even suicidal thoughts. According to a study by the Cyberbullying Research Center, 34% of students who reported being bullied online experienced symptoms of depression, while 19% had suicidal thoughts.

Social media companies have been trying to address the problem of cyberbullying by introducing policies that prohibit bullying and harassment. For instance, platforms like Facebook and Instagram have introduced features that allow users to block and report abusive users. They also work with leading organizations to provide resources and support for those affected by cyberbullying.

Schools and parents also play an essential role in addressing cyberbullying. Many states have enacted anti-bullying laws that require schools to address cyberbullying as part of their anti-bullying policies. Meanwhile, parents can educate their children on proper social media usage, supervise their online activity, and have open communication about their social media experiences.

In conclusion, social media has undoubtedly had significant positive effects on connectivity and communication. However, like all technology, it can also be abused, leading to cyberbullying. The responsibility now rests on social media companies, parents, and schools to work together to combat the rise of cyberbullying and create a safer online environment. It is essential to raise awareness of cyberbullying to prevent its corrosive effects on individuals' mental health and well-being.

THE ROLE OF INFLUENCERS IN SOCIAL MEDIA

Influencers have become a central aspect of social media. They have emerged as a powerful force in the marketing and advertising industry, due to their impact on how people consume and engage with content. An influencer is an individual who has a significant following and may use their platforms to create and share content, usually for brands hoping to promote their products or services. The role of influencers in social media has evolved over the years, and their impact is significant.

In the early days of social media, the influencers were the early adopters of social media platforms, such as bloggers and YouTubers who amassed significant followings based on their niche content. Their audiences respected their opinions and trusted their recommendations, giving them the power to sway purchase decisions. However, as social media platforms developed, the role of the influencer changed. Today, influencers can come in many forms and across different social media platforms.

The emergence of Instagram as a dominant social media platform has been one of the biggest developments in the influencer world. Instagram, with its focus on visual content, has created a space where influencers can share high-quality images and create a strong brand image. Instagram has become the go-to platform for many influencers because it offers an opportunity to get discovered and generate sponsorship deals.

In recent years, brands have recognized the value of partnering with influencers to create content that promotes their products or services. Collaborating with influencers enables brands to reach new audiences and create authentic content, which resonates with consumers. Influencers, on the other hand, have the opportunity to monetize their social media presence and leverage their following to earn an income.

The role of influencers has also expanded to include advocacy and activism. Many social media personalities use their platform to raise awareness about social issues, including climate change, racial justice, and body positivity, among others. They have also been instrumental in amplifying marginalized voices and creating social change.

In conclusion, the role of influencers in social media is significant and has evolved over the years. Influencers have become powerful voices representing their audiences and brands, creating an impact on marketing, politics, and social issues. As social media continues to grow, the influence of influencers is likely to continue on an upward trajectory, shaping the way we consume and engage with content.

THE FUTURE OF SOCIAL MEDIA

As technology advances, social media platforms are constantly evolving to enhance user experience and remain relevant. There are a few notable trends that are already shaping the future of social media:

1. Increased video content - Video content has become more and more popular on social media, with the rise of platforms like TikTok and Instagram Reels. It's becoming clear that video content will play a significant role in the future of social media, as users are captivated by visual storytelling.

2. Augmented reality - Augmented reality (AR) has the potential to transform social media platforms. Snapchat has already pioneered the use of AR filters, but it's expected that other platforms will follow in their footsteps. AR allows users to interact with virtual elements in real-time, and could change the way we communicate on social media.

3. E-commerce integration - Social media platforms like Instagram and Facebook are increasingly integrating e-commerce features, making it easier for users to shop from their favorite brands directly on the app. In the future, e-commerce integration on social media could become even more seamless and customizable, allowing users to make purchases with just a few clicks.

4. Focus on privacy - With growing concerns about data security and user privacy, social media companies will likely continue to prioritize privacy features in the future. There are already platforms like Signal and Telegram that have prioritized privacy, and it's likely that other social media sites will follow suit and enhance their privacy features.

5. Virtual communities - Social media has become an integral part of building communities online, bringing like-minded people together from around the world. In the future, it's likely that social media platforms will continue to foster virtual communities for individuals to connect with one another, share ideas and build relationships.

In conclusion, social media is constantly changing and evolving. While we can make predictions about the future of social media, it's difficult to say exactly what the future will hold. However, it's clear that video content, AR, e-commerce integration, privacy, and virtual communities will play a significant role in shaping the future of social media.

THE IMPACT OF SOCIAL MEDIA ON SOCIETY

Social media has transformed the way people communicate, and it has had a significant impact on society as a whole. With over 4 billion active users worldwide on various social media platforms, it is hard to ignore the influence that social media has on our daily lives. Here are some of the ways in which social media has impacted society.

1. Information dissemination: Social media has become a critical source of information for people worldwide. Social media platforms like Twitter and Facebook allow for instant dissemination of information, breaking news, and live events. Today, people turn to social media for news stories and updates, and major news outlets frequently use social media platforms to keep their followers informed.

2. Enhanced connectivity: Social media has enabled people to connect and reconnect with others worldwide, regardless of geographical location. People can now maintain relationships with friends and family members, even when they are far apart. In addition, social media allows people to interact with like-minded individuals who share similar interests, hobbies and ideas. This has helped build communities of people who would not have otherwise had the opportunity to connect.

3. Democratization of communication: Social media has given everyone with access to the internet the opportunity to have a voice. This has led to the democratization of communication, making it possible for people to share their opinions, ideas, and experiences with a broader audience. Social media has therefore made it easier for individuals to have their voices heard, share

their perspectives and hold others accountable.

4. Changes in culture and language: Social media has created new opportunities for the spread of ideas, culture, and language. Social media has enabled the rise of internet personalities, viral challenges and memes, which have all contributed to shaping the culture and language we use today.

5. Impact on mental health: Social media has both positive and negative impacts on mental health. On the one hand, social media has allowed people to find support and help in coping with mental health issues. However, on the other hand, social media can also have negative impacts on mental health, including increased anxiety, depression, and social isolation.

6. Impact on business: Businesses have had to adapt to the rise of social media, with many now using social media platforms to market products and services. Social media has also allowed businesses to connect with customers directly, respond to their complaints and feedback, and build a loyal customer base.

In conclusion, social media has had a significant impact on society, transforming the way people communicate, interact, and connect with each other. While social media has positives, it is equally important to recognize the potential negative impacts it can have on mental health and other aspects of society. It is essential to use social media responsibly and mindfully to ensure it is a positive force for change.

CONCLUSION: THE HISTORY AND FUTURE OF SOCIAL MEDIA

Social media has come a long way since its early beginnings, with the emergence of websites like Friendster in the early 2000s to the expansive social media networks like Facebook and Twitter that we know today. Through these platforms, people have been able to connect with friends, family members and even strangers across the world, allowing for the creation of new friendships and business opportunities alike.

As social media continues to evolve at a swift pace, it has become clear that these platforms have a major impact on society, for better or for worse. Social media played a crucial role in the Arab Spring uprisings, as activists used platforms like Twitter to mobilize and organize protests across the Middle East. However, social media has also been linked to a rise in cyberbullying, and has been heavily scrutinized by governments for its role in the spread of fake news and propaganda.

One of the biggest changes in social media is the shift towards visual storytelling, led by platforms like Instagram and Snapchat. These platforms have given rise to a new generation of creators, who use social media as a career and as a way to connect with their audience. Influencer marketing has become a major industry, with brands looking to collaborate with social media influencers to promote their products.

As for the future of social media, it is impossible to predict where these platforms will take us. However, it is clear that social media will continue to play a major role in our lives, and it is up to us to determine how we use these platforms. Whether it is to connect with loved ones or to start a business, social media has become an integral part of modern society.

In conclusion, the history of social media is a fascinating one, filled with twists and turns that led to the platforms we know today. As social media continues to evolve, it is important to remember the impact it has on our society and to use these platforms responsibly.

www.ingramcontent.com/pod-product-compliance
Lightning Source LLC
Chambersburg PA
CBHW071118220526
45467CB00004B/1945